Autism Speaks to You from a Teacher's Point of View

By Ethel Williams

Autism Speaks to You from a Teacher's Point of View

A Handbook for Parents

This book can be used by teachers and administrators

A quick reference guide to inform, teach, and empower parents

Your special-needs child can benefit from Ethel Williams' results-

producing classroom methodology, too!

Her completely original approach to educating

the autistic and special-need learner yields dramatic results!

It's okay to feel overwhelmed,

but it's not okay to feel powerless.

Stop worrying . . . Help is on the way!

To order additional copies of this book, contact:
Xlibris Corporation
1-888-795-4274
www.Xlibris.com
Orders@Xlibris.com
74387

CONTENTS

Dedication

I dedicate this book to the many students that I have personally helped to overcome educational, behavioral, and social/emotional challenges. I often think of the students that I have equipped with the knowledge and skills to survive in this ever-changing world. This book is also dedicated to those parents who were lost and confused about a certain diagnosis, and who entrusted their children to me. I wish you love, peace, and happiness. Share these same methods with your family members and friends. The techniques and strategies are the same; only the faces are different.

A SPECIAL THANK YOU

A special thanks to my God and my surrogate families, the Hagoods: Willie Mae, Marion Sr., Debbie and Marion Jr.; the Powdrills: Pearl, R G, Regina, and Karla; the Colstons: Marty, Ingrid, and family; the Emanuels: Bernadine (Bunny), Lona, Sandra, and Lula Mae; the Allens; Janette Smith (co-author of, "The Dangers Of A Stranger") and family. Thanks for including me in your family traditions. To my only living brother, Reverend William Cunningham, his wife Lillian, and daughter Danielle, I wish you love, peace, and eternal happiness. To everlasting friendships, I thank: Vernita Pitts, (whom I have known since middle school), Barbara (BJ) Jackson, Katrina and Katora Cox, Wilma McKinney, Norma and Robert Jones, Denise Fitzhugh and son Everett, Etheldra Williams, Ray Davis, Priscilla Phifer, Leah Myles, Regina Reno, Denise Harris and family, John and Jackie Nichols, Hazel and James Mckeller, Espanita Douglas, (Thanks for encouraging me to follow through.) D'aryl Smith and Dr. Hilda R. Davis.

Some friendships are deemed in heaven, and I believe my friend Ronald Duvall, and his extended family were assigned to me. Thanks for your moral support, Buddy! I couldn't have done this without you. I love you much! To my sister-in-law Jean, my nephews, Anton and Ronnie and my niece Brandi, I wish you all a great life. To Crystal and Diamond Harris, I see great things coming to you, I love you, and I pray that God will bless you in abundance. To Napoleon Quick, Robert and Linda Sibert, and Jan Powell (my confidante) thanks for the great conversation and the laughter.

To my wonderful nieces, Jocylynn and Amber and my nephew Anthony Jr., I pray that life will give you good health, wealth, and a beautiful life. Keep putting God first and education foremost. I love you, and my success is your success! The sky is the limit! Tammy, you have done a wonderful job with my nieces and nephew. Thanks for keeping Anthony Senior's memory alive! If I forgot to mention all the people I love and talk to daily, please forgive me.

WHEN FRIENDSHIP COUNTS

Friends are like sails that inflate in the wind,
They propel you forward, when you're down, or on the mend.
Friends are there when you need them most, never to depart.
Their commitment is relentless, when it comes from the heart!

—Ethel Williams

TESTIMONIAL

Dear Ms. Williams,

Thanks for helping my son Justin. He would keep to himself and was very antisocial. He had problems in reading, memory and writing. The teachers before Ms. Williams would give up on Justin. They would become frustrated and would often suggest that I take him to the doctor for medication. I refused to put my child on medication. I didn't think that was the answer. They thought medicine would keep him focused. I kept on looking for a better solution. I was losing patience and did not know what to do, or where to take him for a real breakthrough. In the fall semester, Justin was assigned to Ms. Williams' classroom at the Burton International School in Detroit Michigan. It was an Early Childhood Developmentally Delayed classroom. Preparing myself for the same discussion, I went into the conference. I was overwhelmed with the feeling of hopelessness. I prepared myself for another nonproductive year. There was something different about Ms. Williams. I tried to explain my discontentment with his previous teachers and schools. No one knew how to educate my child. Ms. Williams listened to every word that I said. Ms. Williams grabbed my hand and looked me straight in the eyes, and said, "You can stop looking. I'm the best that you can find." She asked me to give her a chance to help Justin. I gave her that chance and thank God I did. It was the best thing that ever happened to Justin and me! I kid you not, one month later; Justin began to socialize with the other students. He learned new songs and became excited about learning. He looked forward to going to school. He learned to read, write, and compute math problems. His speech and language skills just exploded. Justin made great friends. He is still in touch with some of his classmates. Justin is currently an A and B student. Ms. Williams gave him the nickname Little Jim Carey, because of his great sense of humor and his ability to sing and dance.

Having Ms. Williams as Justin's teacher was indeed a blessing from God! Not only did she give my son the tools to help him achieve academically, but she also gave me some helpful strategies. I was able to assist my child at home. Thanks to Ms. Williams, my child is on the honor roll. I wish I could have had a teacher like Ms. Williams. I can truthfully say, that when Ms. Williams retired, they lost a gem. She is a legend in her own time.

Thank you,
Jennifer Pelfrey

INTRODUCTION

A Quick Reference Guide

This handbook is designed to provide a quick reference guide for parents of autistic and other special-needs children. A diagnosis of Autism Spectrum, learning disabilities and other social/emotional disorders can sometimes leave parents with a feeling of hopelessness. Sometimes they experience feelings of guilt and failure. My handbook is designed to help parents accept the diagnosis, and find ways to reduce and treat the symptoms. The most important keys to teaching, revitalizing, and rehabilitating the autistic and learning-disabled child are *early detection and early intervention*. This handbook will tell you what to do, when to do it, and how to do it.

Like any other condition, there are levels of severity. The array of symptoms may be different in every child. No one symptom can define an autistic or learning-disabled child. This disability can be as unique as a fingerprint. However, there are certain commonalities that are shared by children exhibiting signs of autism, learning disabilities, and other social/emotional disorders. Most of these disorders are identifiable at a very young age, usually during the first few years of life.

My proven learning techniques and strategies have increased academic growth and improved positive social and emotional behavior in autistic and special-needs students. My methods are derived from years of practice and application, and have often produced desirable results.

This handbook is based totally on the success that I have personally achieved in my classrooms. My classroom management and organizational skills have had a positive effect on teaching and reaching children with autism and other special needs. This handbook will not reflect or discuss other professional or nonprofessional opinions or ideas. It is solely based on my thirty-five years of exemplary teaching experience, my educational preparation, and my proven results.

About Autism Spectrum

The American College of Physicians Complete Home Medical Guide, copyrighted in 1999 and 2003, confirms that autism was first described in 1943. It was defined as a severely impaired development of normal communication and social skills. It affected one in every one thousand children in the United States. The varying levels of autism became known as Autism Spectrum. It was further stated that at least two out of every three children who had confirmed cases of Autism Spectrum had some form of learning disability as well. Some children have a form of autism known as Asperger's disorder. This disorder usually includes children who are academically successful, although they may have poor social skills and/or other limitations. Please check the compiled list of symptoms of autism. (Chapter 13, pg. 66)

Here we are today talking about the same condition that has taken the twenty-first century by storm. Children are being diagnosed with this condition at an alarming rate. Current statistics reveal that one in every 150 children in the United States is being diagnosed with autism. This condition has increased significantly since 1943. The prognosis today may be a little brighter than the initial prognosis when this condition was first identified. Many health-care professionals, educators, and support staff are concerned about the rapid rate in which children are being diagnosed with autism. They have become proactive with devising therapy, learning strategies, educational programs, and creative solutions to help reduce, reverse, and treat the symptoms of autism. To keep consistency throughout this book, I will refer to the varying levels of Autism Spectrum as autism or autistic.

The Diagnosis: How to Cope

Parents are greatly affected when a member of the family has been diagnosed with autism. Yet there are very few resources available to help parents cope.

This handbook will provide some viable options. The autistic child's inability to respond appropriately to social events and learning situations often cause great stress to family members. Some siblings are greatly disturbed by the attention showered on the autistic child. They feel their needs are being neglected. It's hard to have an appropriate balance of time and attention, when one child is so needy.

Parents, you are at the helm. You must seek help to navigate this process effectively. Education and cooperation are needed to illuminate the child. Support groups, community, and family interactions are very important. All family members are needed on deck to help with the illumination process.

The child's feeling of satisfaction and/or accomplishment will always manifest into a smile. My slogan has always been "initiate a smile and illuminate a child." To eliminate ambiguities regarding this slogan referred to in my book, I will define my idea of an "illuminated" child first.

An Illuminated Child

An illuminated child is a radiant child with great self esteem. This child shows a natural age appropriate progression in oral and written communication skills. The child also exhibits adequate physical development, academic achievement and social/emotional growth.

An illuminated child:

> ➤ Exhibits laughter and happiness
> ➤ Exhibits great self esteem (The child feels good about him or herself.)

- Shows age-appropriate progression in academics (The child will master minimal grade level objectives and/or exit skills.)
- Shows adequate social and emotional growth (The child's behavior, social interaction, and emotional development are within the acceptable range.)
- Displays age-appropriate fine and gross motor skills (To develop the gross motor skills the child must exercise the large muscles. The child should be able to walk, run, skip, hop, and jump, like other students or peers in the same age group. The fine motor skills will involve the small muscles, including eye-hand coordination.) *See pp. 29 & 77*
- Incorporates laughter and song into his or her daily routine (The child will become bubbly, happy and enthusiastic.)
- Participates in classroom and group discussions (The child will participate in games and discussions involving two or more people.)
- Shows love towards family members and friends (The child will say words like, "I love you." The child will reach out and touch and actually hug another individual. Signs of affection are commonplace.)
- Begins to communicate appropriately
- Develops age-appropriate vocabulary
- Demonstrates proper speech and language skills (The child's speech pattern, oral and written communication skills will be in an acceptable range.)
- Exhibits age appropriate play and recreation (The child will elicit friends and classmates to engage in age appropriate activities and games.)

CHAPTER 1

A Life-changing Decision

THE WALLS CAME TUMBLING DOWN

In order to protect the integrity of my handbook, I will not discuss any other strategies or methods of instruction used by other educational professionals. This book will only reflect my style of teaching and proven techniques used in my classrooms. I strived to improve the academic achievement of all my students, especially the special-needs child. I personally believe that autism is an old condition with a new emergence. Autism is a term that is used to define or describe various traits or characteristics of a socially, emotionally, and speech/language-impaired child.

My strategies and techniques are solely based on proven results achieved in my classrooms. I will not discuss the position of many dedicated parents in their quest to seek answers about this troubling condition. I can speak only about the progress demonstrated in my classrooms. I can give you two common denominators for my success:

1) My unique style of teaching
2) My organizational skills.

The child's unexplained retreat from the real world has perplexed the best of us. I can only approach this disability from a personal point of view. My personal record can only be measured by the success of the students that I have taught in the last thirty-five years. My strategies and techniques are universally sound. They can be applied at home or in most learning environments. As an educator put in charge of illuminating the child, I had to develop learning strategies, methodologies, and techniques that would ignite the learning process, and reverse the social and emotional alienation. I had to modify unacceptable behavior and get the child ready to learn.

How to Modify Behavior

Behavior modification can be obtained with careful evaluation of the behavior you wish to change, or improve. Positive reinforcement can work wonders. Explain your expectations to your child and together devise a plan of action. Reward your child's small accomplishments with praise and incentives. Continue setting realistic milestones, and eventually your child will achieve your expected results.

With this gigantic responsibility put before me, I became a household name. Many parents in the community were requesting my services. They knew my track record and wanted me to oversee their child's learning plan. Teaching was a natural ability, a gift from God. It was not unusual for me to have taught several members of the same family.

Equipped only with my educational preparation and the gift of teaching, I began my journey to reach and teach all children, especially the special-needs child. I was never satisfied with showing growth in only 99 percent of my students. I was more concerned about the 1 percent who didn't master the skills or objectives. I was sure that there were certain teaching styles and/or modalities that would allow some degree of success in every child. Even the severely learning-challenged child should experience some success.

The questions were: How do I ignite the learning process in the lowest one percent? How do I choose the right modality? How do I apply the right strategies to pique the interest of every child?

Initially, I had to find out whether they were visual, auditory, and/or tactile learners. Sometimes, it takes a combination of all three modalities, visual, auditory and tactile, to ignite the learning process. I was determined to unlock the door that prevented the learning and socialization of all my students. I was the key that made the difference. I developed materials and found creative ways to remediate the lessons for the bottom one percent. My step-by-step handbook for parents will give you some much-needed information and survival skills. I will reveal how I reduced, revitalized and reversed the symptoms of autism in the majority of my students.

Unlike many other teachers, I welcomed the academically, socially and emotionally challenged children. I take great pride in reducing and greatly improving the initial diagnosis. I believe every child can learn. I used to have an expression that described my ability and my passion for teaching a child to read. It went like this, "Bring me a brick and I will teach it to read." My confidence level was off the chart. I had managed to measure some degree of achievement in every child. I knew I could save many children from the fate of their current diagnosis. With time and patience, a new child emerged—a child who developed confidence and skills. I never shied away from situations or students who seemed to be impossible to reach and teach.

However, I remember one situation that required lots of prayer. One year, I was given a very exceptional group of children to teach. Most of the children had mild to severe learning and behavior challenges. Some were autistic and had chronic speech and language impairments. Some weren't even potty-trained. They couldn't physically hold a lunch tray or a carton of milk. Somehow, I knew my ability to teach would be measured by this class, not by my past accomplishments.

This was the first time I had attempted to use my proven techniques and strategies on very young children with very limited abilities. These little fragile babies were waiting for a person like me. Even though these students ranged in ages from five to seven years old, their mental ability and fine and gross motor skills were that of toddlers. They also lacked decipherable oral and written communication skills.

They didn't understand basic concepts, nor did they respond to oral directives. I had to really think about accepting this position. Could I really make a difference in the lives of all these needy children? Being a spiritual person, I asked God to direct me and advise me. I needed to know if God thought I could reverse or improve the skills of the students assigned to me in my Early Childhood Developmentally Delayed (ECDD) classroom.

Many of the students had been in similar programs since age three. Some had been diagnosed at birth. I questioned my effectiveness. I had never tested my system on children so young, so fragile, and so disabled. I even told the principal to pencil me in. I really didn't know whether I could make a difference in children who were so chronically disabled. They all had major speech and language impairments. Some were socially challenged and had some form of learning disability.

My principal was such an understanding, devoted, and perceptive man. He knew he had hired the right person for the job, but he did not pressure me to take on such an enormous responsibility without soul-searching and plenty of prayer.

My success rate and reputation had preceded my arrival, and my track record was at stake. I knew the students were very low functioning.

As I began to read the Individualized Educational Plan (IEP) for each student, I began to understand why God sent me to this school. I examined my abilities again. I became more and more optimistic. I reflected on my successes in my kindergarten classes and the upper levels as well. My teaching experience included grades K-12. I questioned my reluctance. Was this hesitation directly related to the low-functioning level of each student?

Many more questions bombarded my mind. What was different about this challenge? Where would I get the strength to reach deep within to pull out the necessary tools to ignite the souls of God's most needy children?

As I contemplated returning to my previous position, I continued to read the IEPs. God kept evoking thoughts into my spirit. I have never been one to be defeated. That was one of my strong characteristics. I could be defined by my determination and my non-defeatist attitude. I have always developed methods and strategies to improve and ignite the learning process. Why was I skeptical this time?

I needed to completely understand the disability of each child before the next morning. Suddenly, a reality set in! I became enchanted with the names of the majority of the students assigned to my classroom. It was as if the Lord had given me an assignment from heaven. God reassured me that my assignment was not inconsequential; it was designed and sanctioned by Him.

I only had twelve students assigned to my classroom. I reflected on Joshua's battle in Jericho. I immediately started singing quietly to myself, recalling Joshua's determination and stamina. "Joshua fought the battle of Jerico, Jerico, Jerico, Joshua fought the battle of Jerico, and the walls came tumbling down!" Oh what a revelation! Oh what peace I felt as I sang and hummed the lyrics of that song. God was speaking to me through the lyrics and the names of each student. Did he send them to me to be saved from their fate and/or diagnosis? A peace came over me. My conflicted emotions began to slowly dissipate.

Somewhat encouraged, I thoroughly read each and every IEP file. I discovered an array of disabilities that ranged from Attention Deficit Disorder (ADD), Attention Deficit Hyperactive Disorder (ADHD), Emotionally Impaired (EI), Autism (AI), Asperger's Disorder, Crouzon's Disease, Epilepsy, mildly to severely Cognitively Impaired (CI), and Speech and Language Impaired and/or delayed. Also included in this group were students who had been chronically ill, and students who had implanted brain and stomach shunts.

My room was like a melting pot or "hodgepodge" of many different disabilities. My job was to sort out and design an individualized educational plan that would be most effective and productive for each student. Not only did I have the responsibility of illuminating all my students, but I also had to keep them safe and out of harm's way.

I continued to pray and ask God if I were ready for this challenge. Some had been in special programs before age three. They were young, and their functioning level was about half of their chronological age. Their disabilities were so profound. I was prompted to take yet another look at each IEP. I took very precise notes. I thought I could find something different the second time around. This time, I looked for commonalities and possible oversights in the case studies and recommendations for each student. Even then, I was seeking an excuse to return to my previous position.

With one foot on the threshold of the exit door, and one foot in the ECDD classroom, I started to repeat the names of my students. I started to connect and understand why the Lord appointed me to this position. Every name evoked a proverb or a divine intervention. God was telling me something. God chose me to lead his children out of the darkness of disability into the light of ability.

I finally made my decision! I firmly accepted the challenge. Ready to take the lead, body and soul, in the ECDD classroom, I started humming and then singing out loud, "Joshua Fought the Battle of Jericho." As I sang my battle song, a few students started singing with me. How wonderful! Some students were prompted to sing; others just smiled and bobbed their heads. I repeated the chorus, "And the walls came tumbling down, and the walls came tumbling down." I shouted again! "And the walls came tumbling down." My excitement building, I sang with a determination and a commitment. Slowly but building in intensity in a concerto with my students, I ended with a loud burst of energy: "And-the-walls-came-tumble-ling-down!" How significant, how timely, how affirming!

From that point on, I was compelled to do whatever I could to save God's precious gifts. I was hooked and committed to breaking down the barriers that interfered with the learning, social, and behavioral modification process in very young children. Just like Joshua, I was determined to chisel away at the walls that prevented the learning process. I had the task of illuminating the child. Not only was I prepared for the challenge, but also confident that I could accomplish my mission.

The very next morning, I met with the principal. I informed him, that after careful consideration and lots of prayer, I had decided to remain at his school. He could now write my name in ink! The rest is history. I was able to help most of the students in a significant way. Many of my students went on to regular education classes, and did very well.

God knew I was ready for the challenge. I just had to convince myself that I was ready by seeking God's wisdom and confirmation.

CHAPTER 2

My First Day in My ECDD Classroom after My Decision to Accept the Position

THE EXTREME MAKEOVER

My first day in the classroom, after making a life-changing decision, was full of amazement and surprises. Students were unruly, and the classroom was in disarray. Children were running out of the classroom and babbling with an uncontrollable vigor.

The behavior was unacceptable, and learning was minimal. They couldn't write or color. Their fine motor skills were very impaired. The gross motor skills were awkward and clumsy. Even then, they were disruptive and nonproductive. Most of them refused to respond to any oral directives, whether instructional or behavioral. They ran around the room as if to say, this is what we do, and this is all that we do.

The emergency substitute teacher volunteered to stay a few days to familiarize me with the daily routine. I politely told her that it would not be necessary. I told the principal that I didn't need her assistance. I was a Master Teacher, and I knew the sun would come out tomorrow. I knew tomorrow was going to bring some drastic changes. After all, I had just witnessed a very disorderly classroom. Even rest time had been chaotic.

During rest time, the students babbled and played continuously from the cots that were randomly placed on the classroom floor. No one attempted to get order in the classroom. The students were truly in control. I observed this behavior without any input. I wanted to see just how far they would go, and just how much instructional time was actually used for learning.

My observations left me with many questions. When the day was over, I could not believe that no real learning had taken place. The substitute teacher had given me excuses about the students' attention span and their inability to learn. I listened, but I didn't believe her assessment.

My work was cut out for me. I knew I needed to first modify the unacceptable and noncompliant behavior. I had to change the learning environment. There were tables full of unsightly papers. The bulletin boards were dull and lacked stimuli. The furniture was chipped, antiquated and uncoordinated. My classroom needed a face-lift an extreme make over.

My students needed an instructional plan of action, with a defined behavior modification component. I needed to evaluate each and every student. I wanted to find out the true academic levels of all the students. I needed to find out what was really going on with each student. I needed to know what they understood and what they didn't understand. I needed to know their likes and their dislikes. I needed to develop my own plan of action—a plan that was as unique as each student I was assigned to service.

Understanding the mechanics of learning is essential. Especially when developing and implementing a learning and behavioral plan.

Well, let's take first things first. My case studies revealed some very disturbing and interesting data. This information was buried deep within each child's file folder and was available to every special education teacher and support staff. Had anyone ever bothered to read the case studies? I did, and I took good notes. I studied each file. Here are some of my findings:

- Some parents had not potty-trained their child, due to the child's inability to understand the process of eliminating waste.
- Some parents had very limited parenting skills.

- Some parents had engaged in substance abuse during pregnancy.
- Some children had major birth defects, such as cerebral palsy, Crouzon's disease, epilepsy, brain and stomach disorders, and much more.
- Most of the students were full-term babies. A few had pre-mature births.
- 100 percent of the students had been assigned a speech and language therapist for a delay in one or both of the categories.
- 50 percent of all the students had chronic behavior problems, and for these students, a social worker had been requested. Assertive discipline was suggested, but had not been enforced. (See glossary)

Description

Assertive discipline means exactly what it says. You must be firm with your discipline. The child must know that there are consequences for noncompliant behavior. Punishment and consequences must be discussed, predetermined, and enforced. When behavior is not corrected, it empowers the child to continue down the path of disobedience and destruction. If a child throws a ball and breaks a window, after being cautioned and no punishment and consequences are expected or administered, then many more windows will be broken. Remember to enforce realistic and age-appropriate consequences and or punishment! Never abuse or over-punish a child. Taking a favorite toy away, or using a time out period is just as meaningful. As a parent you can decide.

- Some were socially disconnected and/or maladjusted. They preferred to remain isolated or anonymous.
- Not one could complete an age-appropriate standardized test.
- Not one could write his or her name independently.
- Letter and number recognition was nonexistent.

A large percentage of all the students in my classroom had very poor fine and gross motor skills.

Definition

Gross motor skills: involve the development of the large muscle group; these muscles are used when rolling, crawling, creeping, walking, leaping, running, jumping, hopping, skipping, galloping jumping jacks and other similar activities that involve the neck, trunk, legs and the arms. Large muscle strength is also important in climbing, pushing, hanging, pulling, and other similar activities.

Fine motor skills: involve the development of the small muscle group and eye-hand coordination. These activities are usually performed with your eyes, tongue, feet, toes, fingers, wrist and hands, grasping and releasing writing and eating utensils, small tools, scissors, pencils, pens, crayons, spoons, and forks. Movement such as blinking, focusing, sucking, and releasing are also considered to be fine motor skills.

The majority of my children were well-groomed, and had concerned and caring parents. You couldn't identify or match a child's appearance with his or her disability. They looked normal in every way. They were clean and sparkling from head to toe, but they had some real learning and/or behavioral challenges.

Observe your child's age-appropriate progression in social skills, mental and physical development. Compare your child's social and emotional growth with that of his or her peers. Remember, early detection and early intervention of a learning disability can greatly reduce or reverse the symptoms of your child's disability.

Parents and close family members are usually the first to notice delayed or unusual behavior in their child. Sometimes parents are in denial and try to sweep reality under the rug.

Let's not postpone the inevitable. Getting help early for your autistic child is primary. As you begin the steps to reduce and improve your child's condition, you must be vigilante, knowledgeable, and have enormous faith in the professionals. Even though my book is primarily addressed to the parents of children with autism, we can also apply most of the steps to children with other special needs.

CHAPTER 3

Convenience Is Not Always the Best Option

I have a reputation for reaching the unreachable, and teaching the hard to teach. My philosophy is very simple. I believe that every child can learn. The degree of help may vary, but it must be significant. You must strive to leave with more information and knowledge than when you arrived. That's why it's important to evaluate all the students, and keep track of their progress from the onset. As parents you are encouraged to do the same. An informal method of monitoring your child's progress is mandatory. It gives you a basis for discussion and supplies information about your child's progress or lack of progress.

The alliances I have created with my parents and co-workers have been strong, satisfying, and committed.

I am among the last of the old-school teachers. My commitment to the field of education is enviable. I don't accept defeat. When working with an autistic or special-needs child, you must persevere. You must tear down the barriers that inhibit the learning process and prevent adequate social and emotional growth.

Help for your special-needs child doesn't have to be expensive. This handbook will show you how to help your special-needs child at home. You can reduce the cost of outside help, if you follow my proven results process. The success of my students and their return into the mainstream speaks for itself.

You can achieve amazing results at home by following my proven techniques.

Even though, this book is primarily focused on autistic children. The same techniques can be helpful when working with all special-needs children.

Children appreciate order and assertive discipline. I witnessed firsthand a student who was taken from my classroom to attend another ECDD classroom in his immediate neighborhood. His mother wanted him to go to the neighborhood school with his siblings who were in regular education. She looked forward to the day when he could walk to school, and not take the big yellow bus.

Needless to say, her dream came true, or was it her worst nightmare?

He was transferred to his neighborhood school. Things were not like she had expected. The child was dissatisfied with his displacement and lack of structure. Structure and commitment was a major part of my special education program. His mother told me how unhappy he was with his new classroom. He refused to acclimate. He cried continuously throughout the day. He would not complete any task or assignments.

Finally, the mother came to me and requested his return to my classroom. I cautiously asked, "Is there a problem with your new school?" She started by saying, "My child is accustomed to an orderly classroom, and this new classroom is in total chaos."

The child told his mother, "Ms. Williams wouldn't put up with such foolishness." He went on to say, "The children were running around the classroom, hitting and punching other students. No one was listening to the teacher." He continued by saying, "I need to hear so I can learn." He had been one of my most promising students. I really wrestled with the decision his mother had made to transfer him to his neighborhood school. I knew the decision was based strictly on convenience, and not on the best interest of the child.

Mom pleaded with me to take her child back. The decision was very easy. I knew he needed me. I accepted him back into my classroom after explaining the situation to my superiors. They left the decision totally up to me. I welcomed him back with open arms.

"Out of the mouths of babes" came my realization that classroom management was essential in the learning and behavioral modification process. I knew this anyway, but it was nice to have it confirmed by a student who was wise enough to make such a comparison of two different environments. This student suffered from epilepsy, and he instinctively knew that his health depended upon a teacher who demanded order first.

Children learn best when the environment is conducive for learning and the child's safety and security is first and foremost. Special education is not an excuse for noncompliant behavior. We know that special education classrooms sometimes allow a more lenient interpretation of the Student Code of Behavior policy. Even then, a code of behavior must be adhered to.

During an annual IEP meeting, behavioral goals are just as important as instructional goals. Please note that one cannot be achieved without the other. Learning in a quiet, conducive and orderly environment can give a real boost to educational goals and objectives. Convenience is not always the best option!

Always look for the spark in the eyes of each student. There is a glow in each and every one of us. When you see the spark, the glow, or the light, you know that you have piqued the interest of the child. Use it to bridge the familiar with the unfamiliar, the known with the unknown, the boring with the interesting.

CHAPTER 4

Be Proactive Parents:
Don't Deny or Delay Diagnosis

This chapter will give you some pertinent information on how to become proactive parents. It will tell you how to observe, compare and react to your child's first visible sign/s of delays and/or impairments. This information will help you navigate public education protocol.

Step One: Parental observation and input is essential!

What to do:

- ❖ Observe your total child, take notes, and compare his or her behavior with peers.
- ❖ React to the child's first observable delays in learning, social and physical development.
- ❖ Seek a second opinion from close family members. Have them observe your child. If they share the same conclusion, then schedule an immediate evaluation by a physician or an educational professional. Always remember to compare your child with other children the same age. We know children develop at different rates. However, if your child is displaying significant learning, social and developmental delays, then you must seek help *right away!*

Step Two: Seek early diagnosis and intervention

Before your child starts an educational program, a physical examination is mandatory. This exam will give you an overall picture of your child's physical and emotional health. The examination may reveal that your child is perfectly healthy. It could indicate that your child may have a hearing and/or visual impairment. On the other hand, the physical examination may reveal other areas of concern, such as dyslexia or other disorders of the brain. Whatever the case may be, immediate intervention, knowledge and commitment, will help you get the ball rolling.

❖ Arrange an appointment with your child's pediatrician.

❖ If the child is school age, share your concerns with the child's teacher.

❖ Most public schools have a team of professionals on staff to test and evaluate the students.

❖ More than likely, the teacher has already detected a problem. Together, you can expedite the child's evaluation.

❖ There are private entities that will do the same thing, usually for a fee.

❖ Some hospitals will provide testing and evaluation through your medical insurance.

Throughout the process keep in mind:

❖ As parents, you must insist that the evaluation be swift and intervention immediate. The process can be slow, but you must be patient, yet, persistent!

❖ Remember, time is of the essence. It can be the difference between reducing and reversing your child's symptoms.

❖ Do not be passive! You must be persistent! Time is money. Time can be very valuable to your child's recovery.

❖ Don't hesitate; move swiftly.

❖ Invest your time, dedication, and commitment wisely.

Step 3: Interpret and discuss your child's professional evaluation

Do your homework so you can discuss your child's fate, suggested placement and educational plan effectively.

Remember, knowledge is power!

- ❖ Familiarize yourself with the process, the terminology, the options, and the classification of each disability that may apply to your child. It is important to know the characteristics and description of each category.
- ❖ Do not come to the meeting unprepared! Know your rights, and let the professionals know, that you know your rights.
- ❖ Research the recommendations and give your input and opinions about your child's diagnosis and recommended course of action. This can be a daunting task, but it is necessary. Knowledge is power!
- ❖ Don't be afraid to reach out and ask for assistance to help you understand the terminology. Request an advocate to walk you through the process.
- ❖ Welcome feedback. Listen to all options and test findings. If you need more time and/or an explanation of the findings, you can request further information and a continuance at a later date. This will allow you more time to assimilate the materials and understand the diagnosis. If you decide to reconvene at a later date, move quickly and without delay. Remember, time is very important, and you want time on your side.
- ❖ Always request the school's Special Education Handbook, and Student Code of Behavior Policy. Know all terminologies, categories, definitions and descriptions, for every term used.

Step 4: A Prescription For Learning

The IEP is a legal document and must be treated as such. Preparation and knowledge of the content is very important prior to the IEP meeting. Most states have a similar document in place. The IEP could vary from state to state. Familiarize yourself with your school district's IEP.

❖ What is an IEP? IEP stands for an Individualized Educational Plan. This is a legal document. It can be enforced in a court of law. It will orchestrate your child's annual learning and behavior plan. It will reflect short and long-term learning and behavioral goals and objectives.

Remember to read all recommendations and elements of this document: (IEP)

- ✓ Performance—goals and objectives
- ✓ Instructional—goals and objectives
- ✓ Social/emotional behavioral—goals and objectives
- ✓ Speech and language—goals and objectives
- ✓ Social worker—goals and objectives
- ✓ Transportation options
- ✓ Current personal data, telephone number, address, gender, category, DOB, etc.
- ✓ Eligibility
- ✓ Primary disability category
- ✓ Support staff and team recommendations
- ✓ Current test scores, academic achievement and functional performance levels
- ✓ Least restrictive environment considerations
- ✓ Programs and services determined appropriate to meet the student's needs

- ✓ Additional considerations
- ✓ Extent of service hours (Time spent in special education and regular education programs)
- ✓ Anticipated duration of program and services
- ✓ Commitment signatures
- ✓ Methods of reporting progress

1) Progress reports
2) Report cards
3) Parent/teachers' conferences
4) Annual IEP meeting

The annual IEP meeting must involve the parents, the teachers, the administrators and all support staff. All parties involved with your child's educational plan must sign the final document. It is not the sole responsibility of the Special Education teacher. It is a joint effort and must be reflective of all participating support staff members. Every member of your child's educational team should be present at the annual IEP meeting. If the parents or guardians are not satisfied with the projected IEP, they have the right to refuse to sign the document until they are satisfied. Parents can offer other suggestions and considerations that may result in an agreement that all parties can live with. Sometimes parents fail to sign the IEP because they are in denial about their child's disability. Don't delay! Remember, that time is of the essence in getting help for your child. An unsigned IEP can cause further delays in servicing your child!

When all parties agree with all the components, then, and only then, will the document be signed. After all parties have signed the IEP, it now becomes a legal document, enforceable in the court of law.

If a key member of your IEP team is absent, due to unforeseen scheduling problems or illness, a mini IEP can be conducted to get the input of the absent team member. The parents should attend this meeting as well.

*Special Note:

It is important for the special education teacher to get the IEP invitations out in a timely manner to avoid scheduling problems. Usually thirty days in advance. Several follow-up phone calls in between, to confirm date, time and commitment, is not only appropriate, but also highly suggested.

As parents you must be proactive! You must check to see if all components checked on the IEP have been implemented, enforced, and are ongoing in the designated school year. If the goals and objectives outlined on the IEP, have not been initiated in the year the document was scheduled to be implemented, a legal challenge can ensue. Due Process is your right!

CHAPTER 5

Well-balanced Meals are Essential to Good Health

Prepare healthy meals

I encourage parents to select healthy meals and snacks. Try to choose foods from the six basic food groups. Always consult your pediatrician before any diet is selected. Food allergies and other health risk can alter a child's diet. Only your child's pediatrician will know for sure. Remember, the suggested food pyramid is not customized for your child. Substitute foods and other alternatives are strictly between you and your child's doctor or dietician.

❖ Make sure your child is eating three well-balanced meals, and two to three healthy snacks daily.
❖ Be aware of what your child can or cannot eat. Allergies and food intolerances could be very detrimental to your child's health.
❖ Use the following daily-recommended guidelines when planning meals:
  1. Meat, Eggs, Fish, Nuts and Dry Beans (2-3 Servings per day)
  2. Vegetables (3-5 Servings per day)
  3. Fruits (2-4 Servings per day)
  4. Milk, Yogurt, And Cheese (2-3 Servings per day)
  5. Bread, Cereal, Rice, and Pasta (6-11 Servings per day)
  6. Candies, Cakes and Oils (Minimal Servings)

For more information, see the Healthy Living food pyramid on page 49 of the American College Of Physicians Complete Home Medical Guide, copyrighted

1999 and 2003. David R. Goldmann, MD FACP Editor—In Chief-, David A. Horowitz, MD, Associate Editor. Food pyramid charts will state the recommended daily servings for each food group, with suggested food choices for every category.

Most of the children whom I have serviced in the past have been from low to moderate-income families. The one common factor involving the majority of the children in my classroom, was the fact that 99 percent of them received free lunch. The few students, who were able to purchase or bring a packaged lunch, chose the same or similar menu items. The six major food groups were mainly represented. The children looked forward to their mid-day meal.

No special diet was associated with the free lunch program. Everyone selected food entrees from the same menu. Taste buds were factored into their choices. Children have very finicky appetites. Milk, fruit/fruit juice, bread, vegetables, starch, meat, and dessert, were the standard of the day. The menu represented the six basic food groups. Some were too poor to be selective, and some were too hungry to leave food on their plates. Some children refused to eat the vegetable of the day, no matter how they were presented. Most of the students ate whatever they were given on any particular day. It was a well-balanced diet that was shared and consumed by the entire school. Therefore, I can't say that a particular diet had anything to do with the illumination process. When a child is full and well nourished the healing can begin.

I know some parents are adamant about a gluten-free diet and have eliminated foods containing gluten from their child's daily menu. However, I cannot discuss the gluten-free theory at this particular time, because it was not a factor in my classroom. More studies must be conducted to validate any disputable claims.

The significant learning progress in my classroom can only be attributed to the carefully designed techniques, strategies, and methodologies. I'm not disputing the fact that a gluten-free diet can be helpful. I just don't have enough information to personally support or refute it.

In addition to this, all of my students received all recommended early-childhood immunizations. The effects of childhood immunizations can only be speculated, but not verified at this time. Only the medical professionals can discern the disability, the characteristics associated with it, and maybe one day, pinpoint the origin or cause.

Excess sugar, salt and fat are not recommended for any diet. These foods have been known to contribute to hyperactivity, obesity, tooth decay, diabetes, kidney failure, heart attacks, strokes and other health problems. Try to select foods that are low in sugar, salt and fat content.

Until a cure for Autism Spectrum is found and a more acceptable explanation is given, our only option is to devise programs to reduce and treat the symptoms.

Right now, intensive learning strategies, speech and language development, physical and occupational therapy, social revitalization/rehabilitation and behavior modification programs are being offered and implemented daily. As parents, you can apply many of the same techniques, strategies, and methods used by the medical and educational professionals at home.

By first ensuring that your child's body is well nourished, you are fostering the physical health essential to the success of these teaching tools.

CHAPTER 6

Educating Your Child at Home

Create an environment conducive to learning

This chapter will show you how to utilize space within the home for tutorial sessions.

The learning space could be as simple as a chair at the kitchen table. It could be a designated area in the far corner of the living room. Or it could be as extensive as an entire room that has been converted into a classroom within the home.

Make sure:

- The learning environment is quiet and clutter free.
- You design a classroom or designate a learning space for your child, within your home. This area must be clean organized and used specifically for that purpose.
- Age-appropriate learning charts, posters, and other stimuli are displayed throughout the learning space.
- Early-childhood students have charts that display name, numbers, letters, calendar, seasons, phonics, handwriting formation, sight vocabulary, and storybooks.
- Flash cards, with age-appropriate information are utilized daily.
- Colorful mobiles are infused throughout the learning environment.

Activities to emphasize in your learning environment

Laughter is mandatory in the illumination process.

Always:

- Include activities that will enhance and develop fine and gross motor skills daily. (See glossary for a complete list)
- Use plenty of nursery rhymes and songs. (Children love to sing and learn through songs, poems, and prose.)
- Make happy music and dance moves a part of your daily routine.
- Encourage exercise and extension of all the large muscles daily. (See glossary under gross motor skills)
- Encourage exercise and extension of all the small muscles daily. (See glossary under fine motor skills)
- Encourage your child to laugh and coo. (This will stimulate the child's vocal cords and familiarize the child with sounds that will eventually lead to speech.)
- Encourage laughter and fun activities.
- Devise goals based on the child's ability.
- Review age-appropriate information daily. (New and old information)

Children learn best in an orderly environment or space. Confusion and disarray bring negative or, at best, minimal results. If you do not have a designated learning area in your home, consider adding something educational to each room of your home. Thus, the whole house becomes a classroom. Your special-needs or autistic child is worth the sacrifice.

CHAPTER 7

How to Organize Your Time for Best Results

This chapter will tell parents how to allot time for specified learning
sessions.

Key Concepts:

Schedule time for working together every day

Involve the whole family

Emphasize repetition, routine, and responsibility

The time you commit to your child at home can have phenomenal results.
It can also save you a truckload of money. Time, commitment, and
dedication are not expensive, but they must be budgeted and executed
efficiently and daily.

Consider doing the following:

➢ Block out the time you are at work. Find a daily time that can
be delegated to you and your special-needs child. Scheduling is
key. Don't assume that only one person can help the autistic and
special—needs child. Involve the whole family in engaging your
special-needs child, with, perhaps, one person primarily responsible
for daily learning sessions.

To increase success the following should be considered:

- ➤ Select a designated time for learning.
- ➤ Designate a specified area for learning.
- ➤ Be consistent with the daily time or routine.
- ➤ Select daily objectives from the IEP to zero in on. Include reinforcement of the teacher's daily objectives and homework assignments. (Parents will have a copy of the IEP)
- ➤ Review and repeat weekly and monthly objectives, daily.
- ➤ If the child is not school age, then you may want to get a developmental progression chart from your pediatrician.
- ➤ Daily tactile (hands-on), visual, and auditory stimulation is mandatory.
- ➤ Make sure the learning space is used primarily for your child's study time, drills and daily learning sessions.
- ➤ Repetition, routine and responsibility are applied daily.
- ➤ Find what sparks your child's interest. (Does he or she respond favorably to electronic games, computers, toys, music and songs?)
- ➤ Retention and mastery occur because of repetition and routine. For example, count from one to one hundred daily, even if the child can count. Find something different to add, but continue to count. Ask the child to point to the number 10, or some other number for variation and reinforcement. Never stop counting.
- ➤ If your daily routine includes one-on-one tutoring and stimulation from six to seven o'clock, please try to avoid doing other things. This time has been allotted, and don't let anything get in your way.
- ➤ The more time you devote to the illumination process, the better your results will be.
- ➤ Devotion and commitment are ongoing. It's not just one hour a day. You must apply all techniques and strategies throughout the day, whether it's in the supermarket or the church. Keep your eyes on your prize.
- ➤ When you get up in the morning, rehabilitation begins. A big hug, a kiss, or a smile is not only therapeutic, but it helps to wake up one's emotions. To ignite the social interactions of children, they must first feel and see the emotion daily.

➤ If your child appears to retreat into him or herself and prefers to be alone as opposed to interacting with family members and attending age-appropriate social gatherings and games, seek help right away.

➤ Tickle the stomach or add some other types of stimulation; eventually the child will respond and/or react.

➤ Never attempt to give less than an hour per day, even if it means deviating from a stringent routine. Change the scheduled time, but never give up. You cannot cancel the lesson, the discussion, or the activity. Flexibility can be an option. Try very hard to stick to your original time frame. Remember, a child likes structure and routine. Try to make your lessons a little more interesting, but don't quit until its time to end the session.

C H A P T E R   8

How to Increase Your Autistic Child's Communication Skills

This chapter will help your autistic and special-need child communicate sooner.

- Children with impaired and/or delayed speech must be encouraged to speak or verbally communicate their thoughts and wants.

  Most school districts have speech and language therapists on board to work with your speech and language-impaired and/ or delayed child. Parents can be very effective at home. Just by initiating daily conversations. Do not allow a child to point if speech is within his/her realm. You must insist on the child asking for what he/she wants, especially if the child is at the age where speech is a part of the age appropriate developmental progression.

- Encourage the child to speak in complete sentences.

  If the child is nonverbal, the person in charge should continue to speak, as if it were a two-way conversation, even if the conversation is one-sided. Eventually, the child will hear and understand the relevance and mechanics of conversation.

- Give your child a reason to speak.

  During your adlib conversation, say things that would be completely false or erroneous. A questionable or contrary response will often lead to an expression of discontentment. This discontentment will sometimes promote a frustrated facial expression that someday will accompany a verbal rebuttal. Remember, we're looking for avenues to spark the verbal responses.

- Facial expressions can sometimes give you visual clues to the child's understanding of concepts and the English language.

  For example, if you know that a child hates spinach and your conversation reflects your child's love for the hated vegetable, usually an outward expression of disgust, rejection or disapproval will appear. Eventually, the child will not only show a visible response to incorrectness, but will also begin to refute the claim with words.

- The first real words may be immature and indecipherable, but an attempt was made to clarify and/or justify the situation or the encounter. Be patient, yet hopeful, a breakthrough is imminent.

- Vocabulary cards with colorful pictures are also very motivating.

  Present the picture with the new vocabulary word. The child's mind is speaking within. Eventually, the child will begin to mimic and say the word or words verbally. Progress will be slow but significant.

- Parents should have similar conversations and vocabulary development sessions throughout the day.

  o The grocery store is another good arena to have great conversation with your child. Familiar foods and beverages will stimulate a child's curiosity and participation in the purchase of foods and beverages that he or she likes.

o The zoo or age-appropriate field trips will prompt visual and verbal exchanges. Animals have always been a child's best friend. Family recreation, dinner parties, and other family functions are all igniters of conversation and fun activities.

o Age-appropriate movies and plays will captivate a child's imagination and will elicit conversation.

o While driving home, involve your speech-delayed and language impaired child in conversation. He/she may respond with facial clues, visual gestures, or premature language. Whatever venue he or she uses to respond is better than none at all.

- Always make some contradictory statements that will make your speech-delayed or impaired child react or think.

For example, Susie lives next door in the pink house. The child knows that Susie lives across the street in the blue house. The child will know better and will eventually try to relay the true statement, either at that moment or at a later date.

- Always include the child with the impairment (delayed and nonverbal speech) into the conversation.

Don't use their limited verbal skills to excuse or exclude them from the conversation or social activity.

- Encourage conversation with flash cards.

Vocabulary and language development flash cards are helpful tools to promote mental and physical interactions. Sometimes a picture with a word attached or underscored is ideal. For example, a picture of an apple with the word *apple* visibly displayed will cause a mental notation and a physical connection to the fruit. A bowl of fruit nearby can cause the child to reach for the newly discovered fruit. This will trigger an association between the word and the picture.

Further conversations can be initiated from that single piece of fruit. The parent, the teacher or the speech and language therapist can link other unique situations and experiences to that same piece of fruit. For expansion, ask the child if he or she likes apples. What about apple pie? What about candy apples? Use as many avenues as possible to ignite the communication and language development process.

Don't forget to use taste, touch and smell to spark recognition and conversation. The same techniques can be used to expand conversations and reactions to other situations.

CHAPTER 9

How to Increase Your Child's Writing Skills

This chapter will help parents develop the writing skills in their autistic and special needs child.

Increasing your child's writing skills can be as simple as practice and constructive modeling. Never leave your child alone to complete a writing assignment without precise instructions and modeling. It could be as simple as connecting the dots to make an uppercase A or as difficult as writing a short paragraph or report. Either one of the assignments can be challenging if the child has no clue as to how to get started.

The objective of the day may center on the proper way to hold a pencil or other writing utensils. Sometimes we have to take a step backward in order to establish a firm foundation. Remember if the foundation is weak, the skills will be weak. Rebuild the foundation and the child will begin to flourish.

Your child's lack of age-appropriate writing skills doesn't necessarily mean that there's a real deficit in that area. It may be a physical impairment that can easily be corrected with glasses and/or other minimal restrictive accommodations. It could also mean that the child didn't have a clear understanding of the task at hand.

Getting started with developing writing skills involves some simple techniques:

- The early-childhood student should learn how to trace sticks and circles. After mastery of tracing sticks and circles, the child should be able to make sticks and circles independently. Sticks and circles are the basic fundamentals of manuscript writing.

- Always start with the upper case letters first.

The lowercase letters can be introduced at the same time, but I suggest you concentrate on the formation of the uppercase letters first. Feel free to introduce a new letter daily. Explain the mechanics of forming the letter "*A*", two slanted sticks and one short stick in the middle. The lowercase letter "*a*" is made with a circle and a stick. You can teach your child how to form every letter of the alphabet.

Invest in handwriting books for your younger learner. Make sure letter tracing and manuscript writing are represented. Most handwriting books geared towards primary learners usually dedicate several pages for introduction, formation and practice of letters A-Z, and numbers 1-10. These books also include isolated words and short precise sentences.

There are more advanced handwriting books for the more capable students. Cursive writing may be displayed and formatted in this book, along with more complex sentence-structure and paragraph—writing skills.

- Use standard 1G paper.

This paper has wider spaces between lines and is usually color-coded. If the child's ability is too immature for lined paper, a plain white sheet of paper is recommended. Start with 1G paper when the child's spacing awareness is evident. Advance to 2G paper after the child has mastered spacing. These lines are closer together. More advanced writers can use regular loose-leaf paper with margins.

- Make sure your child is acutely aware of the spacing used for upper- and lower-case letters.

- Parents, you must purchase a letter chart that shows the proper way to form manuscript letters. This is essential. If you make the letters wrong, then you are modeling the wrong letter formation to your child. The child will emulate whatever you model, be it right or wrong.

- Always write your child's name at the top of the page in the proper space and model the correct formation. Always leave a space underneath the modeled name for the child to practice writing his or her name at least five times.

- Start with the first name for the first few months, and then start to model the first and last name around the third or fourth month.

- Display your child's name throughout the room. Tape your child's name on his/her desk and in various locations within the home. Your child should be able to recognize and eventually spell and write his/her name independently.

- Spacing in not important at the initial modeling session. You can explain the mechanics, but don't criticize the child, if he or she is having problems with spacing.

- Children should practice writing their name as soon as they are able to hold a writing instrument. Children may show a serious attempt to write their name, even if the spacing is off. Spacing will come later.

- Older children, who have mastered letters, spacing, and formation, may start copying sentences from the board, black lined master sheets, or handwriting books, until they are confident enough to form sentences on their own.

- Older children will eventually add a sentence of their own. When they can devise sentences independently, it's okay to help them with the spelling of some or all of the words.

- Emphasize phonics skills when trying to spell words the child would like to use.

  If the word is *book*, ask the child to listen and identify the letter associated with the initial sound of the word. Next, ask the child to listen to the end sound of the word and repeat the process. He may or may not come up with the right letter or letters. The important skill at this time is coming up with a complete thought. Continue nurturing and modeling the writing process. Eventually, forming a sentence will be commonplace: *The ball is red. The girl is pretty. I like to run.*

- Use some sight words in your daily sentences.

  This will expand vocabulary development; enhance the understanding of new concepts, spelling skills, and sentence structure. Drawing pictures to depict the designated sentence is very helpful in comprehension and understanding.

- Understanding simple sentence structure will soon develop into writing short stories and paragraphs.

- Be patient and know when to advance to the next level. Always repeat learned objectives and then expand and explore new territory.

- Display or keep a writing folder that shows your child's progress in the writing process. Children get excited about seeing their work displayed on the wall and other designated areas.

Remember to model all writing assignments.
For more advanced students remember to model thinking out loud in deciding what to write.

CHAPTER 10

How to Teach Your Child to Read

This chapter will teach parents how to start the reading process.

A child's ability to read is a natural booster to his or her self-esteem and success.

Reading starts at infancy. Understanding object and word associations start at an early age. A child recognizes his bottle long before he can say or identify the word in print. When your child exits the womb, reading begins. Your child begins to recognize your face, your smell, your touch, and your kiss. She knows when she is soothed by a stranger or by her biological parents. She is aware of the attention-getting sounds. It can be as discreet as a constant whimper, or as loud as a bone-chilling scream. She knows how to demand and command attention.

Starting the Reading Process

Always link a word to an object or person. Never think a child is too young to associate relationships. Point to pictures and objects and say the names out loud. This will eventually increase the child's vocabulary and knowledge base. You will be amazed to know what the child is retaining.

- **Read to your child daily:**

   Point to pictures and objects daily. This will eventually increase the child's vocabulary development and understanding. Always discuss the content of the short story or the picture book with your child. If the child is old enough, check for comprehension; if not, just read for enjoyment and exposure.

   Don't let a day go by without reading to your child. Reading is the most important gift you can give your child. Promote conversation and understanding of the book or short story. This is a good way to get your child to communicate. If your child can read, ask your child to read to you. If your child cannot read, you must read to your child. Allow your child to read and enjoy the pictures within the pages daily. This is a must! Discuss the content of the story with your child. Ask questions that will demonstrate comprehension. Beginners can interpret the pictures.

- Alphabet recognition skills

   Children should be able to sing and recite the alphabet song before they exit kindergarten. My recommendation is to start this process during the preschool years. Start by teaching the letters in your child's name, continue with the letters of the alphabet. An alphabet chart is suggested. Visuals are very helpful with memory retention. During this process, remember the three Rs: repetition, routine, and responsibility.

The Three Rs

Repetition: Review learned objectives and introduce new objectives daily.

Routine: Use the same method or format daily. Children like routine, expectation and anticipation.

Responsibility: Pro-actively involve your child in learning, homework, and behavior modification.

- **Phonics skills:**

The child should be able to identify the vowel letters (AEIOU), and the consonants, which are the remaining letters of the alphabet. The child should be able to discriminate the sound each letter makes. Advanced students should recognize rhyming words, word families, and syllables. Decoding skills will manifest when your child has mastered phonetic skills.

Word Families: cat, fat, rat. dog, log, hog

Rhyming Words: mouse-house

Syllables: good*bye (2); thank*you (2)

Students should be able to group words that are similar in meaning and words that are opposite in meaning.

Please purchase grade level phonics book or books. You won't regret it! Phonetic progression is outlined in every book. (Beginners, Intermediate, an Advanced)

- **Decoding skills**

Children should be able to decode words with one or more syllables, after mastery of the phonics component. Phonics is the key to unlocking the correct enunciation and pronunciation of the English language (d - o - g (*d* sound + Short *o* sound + hard *g* sound = dog)

- **Sight words**

Flash cards showing sight words should be displayed throughout the room. The ultimate goal is to have the sight vocabulary words ingrained in your child's memory bank. Daily drills and flash cards are essential to your child's success. Remember, repetition, routine, and responsibility should help your child master age-appropriate vocabulary words.

Encourage your child to copy or create simple sentences using the new or daily sight words. Flash cards are recommended. For example: you can introduce and display the words *the, you, red, and, look, see, green, yellow, can, run, jump, boy, girl, and dog* daily. Add new words when your child has mastered the old ones.

Make sure all the words you introduce can be used to make sentences. For example:

Vocabulary List
boy

girl

jump

the

can

run

The boy can run.

The girl can jump.

- **Punctuation marks:**

Introduce punctuation marks (. ? !). Explain the role of each punctuation mark and its effect on good sentence structure. Ask the students to make up sentences and questions using the appropriate punctuation mark. Commas and quotation marks will be introduced next. If your child is unable to write his or her own sentence, find various sentences within the story to discuss end punctuation marks.

A sentence that tells you something - **(.)** must end with a period.

A sentence that ask a questions - **(?)** must end with a question mark.

A sentence that shows strong feelings or emotions must end with an **(!)** exclamation point.

CHAPTER 11

How to Introduce Math Concepts to the Very Young

This chapter will encourage parents to use visuals and hands-on materials when teaching the autistic and special-needs child.

> **Teach all subjects with the same dedication and vigor. It doesn't matter whether the subject is spelling or world history. It's not the subject that determines mastery; it's the dedication, the commitment, the techniques, the strategies, and the methods outlined in this book that make the difference.**

Children are mainly visual, auditory, and tactile (the sense of touch) learners. Always provide number charts, flash cards, and manipulatives, during the learning sessions.

Counting to ten is always a good start for the young child. Do not add to your ten-count until your child has achieved mastery in both recognition and oral counting. You can teach quantity simultaneously but don't over crowd the lesson. Introduce visual quantity in a leisurely fashion with the selected number daily. Do not overwhelm the child.

Even when your child has achieved mastery, only add an additional number and quantity when you think the child is ready to move on.

Math can be fun! Count items that are familiar and fun like candy pieces. Find fun things to count in the classroom or learning environment. Just count daily.

Have a number line and a 1-100 number chart displayed throughout the learning space. Give the child the pointer and let the child lead the counting session.

Purchase age-appropriate math books for daily drills and fun activities. If the child is unable to complete the activity, after careful and precise interactive instructions, feel free to complete the sheet with the child. Remember to repeat the same sheet at a later date, when your child has a better understanding of the objective. The child may be able to complete the sheet independently. If not, patience and steadiness is always the answer.

Also encourage your child to count household items. The possibilities are endless. Think cereal, pasta, cookies, spices and bottles of pop as examples of things you can count.

Introduce other math concepts when the child has mastered number recognition and quantities from one to twenty-five.

- Introduce the plus (+) sign.
- Introduce the minus (-) sign.
- Introduce the equal (=) sign.
- Pair all computations with visual clues and manipulatives. Use cubes, straws, or other small object to visually compute and reinforce the concept.
- Never teach math to a young child without visuals and manipulatives. Use small objects to visualize and reinforce the concept.
- Counting fingers is an acceptable mode of learning. It helps the child visualize the number and the quantity.
- Don't move to subtraction until your child completely understands addition.
- Advance when understanding is evident.
- Make sure your child can count to one hundred.

- Counting should be taught in intervals of ten: one to ten, one to twenty, one to thirty, one to forty, one to fifty, one to sixty, one to seventy, one to eighty, one to ninety, all the way to one to one hundred.

Also note: There are several charitable non-profit organizations that will provide equipment, supplies and monetary grants to parents of autistic and special-needs children. Check your local and national directories for this information. **Do your research!**

RECAP: CHAPTER 12

How to Teach Your Autistic and Special-needs Child

This chapter will highlight the information given earlier.

✓ **Repetition**

- Develop the fine and gross motor skills daily.
- Read to your child daily.
- Require your child to point to every word when reading to you.
- Listen to your child read daily.
- Promote daily conversations.
- Engage in age appropriate writing assignments daily.
- Check comprehension skills by asking questions.
- Encourage daily socialization activities.
- Demonstrate word awareness, proper reading progression and word order. Determine whether a child is reading from left to right or right to left. This is very important when teaching your child to read.
- Teach sight and vocabulary words daily. Post words throughout the room or learning space. Use flashcards to drill sight words into your child's memory bank.
- Teach your child familiar jingles, songs and rhymes.

✓ Routine

- Make sure the learning area is quiet and orderly.
- Use the same format daily.
- Be consistent with your time frame.
- Organize your time for best results.
- Bridge the known with the unknown.
- Socialize your autistic and special-needs child.

✓ Responsibility

- Trigger interest in learning. Make learning fun.
- Ignite the memory process.
- Apply assertive discipline.
- Devise a behavior modification plan.
- Instill responsibility in your child
- Insist on proper rest and good sleep habits.
- Make sure your child has at least three well-balanced meals per day and two or three healthy snacks.
- Use visuals and manipulatives when teaching math
- Initiate a smile and illuminate a child.

CHAPTER 13

Denial Prolongs The Inevitable

This Chapter is designed to help parents recognize
the symptoms of autism.

When to Do It: Right Now!

Denial prolongs the inevitable. Testing, observation and evaluation should
be immediate. It is proven that the earlier you start an intervention program,
the quicker you can start your child on the road to recovery. Knowing what
to do, how to do it, and when to do it, can hasten a breakthrough. If your
child exhibits the symptoms listed below, don't delay. Get help today.

Symptoms of Autism

The child:

➤ Has a distant stare
➤ Is emotionally detached
➤ Never volunteers to hug, kiss or cuddle with parents
➤ Lacks sparkle and enthusiasm
➤ May or may not complete an assignment
➤ Plays with the same toy every day and ignores other toys
➤ Has an imaginary playmate or friend
➤ Dominates free time with special interest toy/s (If the child
loves to build, he/she will seek the same building blocks
every day.)

- May salivate when talking
- Is very anti-social, reluctant to make friends, and prefers to be alone and anonymous
- May blurt out curse words or other disturbing sounds or phrases
- Will not stay focused
- Speaks gibberish
- Repeats the question in response to a question. For example, What color is the apple? Answer: What color is the apple?
- Is unable to answer questions that require oral or written communication and comprehension skills
- May go to sleep during recess or classroom activities
- Prefers not to participate in group discussions
- Tends to forget information that was once a part of his knowledge base (the child used to count to twenty, but now doesn't count at all)
- Academic achievement and social/emotional growth are greatly compromised
- Replaces joy and laughter with a lost and stoic expression
- Is not amused with baby talk or any efforts to get his or her attention
- Has delayed speech and language skills
- Fine and gross motor skills are awkward and under developed
- Lacks excitement and active participation in family activities
- Lacks eye contact
- Social and emotional behaviors are retreating
- Prefers not to participate in group activities
- Lacks confidence
- Displays moderate and violent outbursts and temper tantrums
- May display aggressive behavior toward other students and adults

If your child displays one or more of the above symptoms, please seek help today.

Initiate a smile . . . Illuminate a child!

This information was presented early on in this handbook, but it is so vitally important that it bears repeating here. Ignoring your child's first observable signs of possible autism could greatly increase your child's chances of having a permanent condition.

The first step in helping your autistic child is to recognize the symptoms associated with your child's condition. Make notes of all questionable and disturbing behavior, even if it's not listed on the above symptoms of autism chart. Share results with other family members to see if their observation is consistent with yours. Remember, early diagnosis and immediate intervention are critical to your child's future! Don't delay if you suspect a slight problem. Face your gut feeling right away. Time is not on your side.

Have your child evaluated by a medical or educational professional right away. Proceed as directed. Time, devotion, dedication, and commitment are essential to teaching, socializing, revitalizing and rehabilitating the autistic and special-needs child.

I am the last of the old-school teachers. I believe learning and behavior goals should be reflective of your child's ability. Some parts of the lesson should be simple enough for the challenged learner and complex enough to challenge the learner.

CHAPTER 14

A Child's Mind Rebounds With Amazing Vigor!

Everyone Should Be Able to Experience Success!

We are all teachers by nature. Some are teachers by professional choice. Whatever the case may be, this handbook will tell you how to blend your special talent and skills, to augment your child's education at home. **Don't delay start today!**

Special Education teachers are trained to write individualized lesson plans. Hopefully, I have empowered you as parents to write mini plans to help your child at home. Feel free to get suggestions from your child's teacher. The feeling of satisfaction and accomplishment is the same; they both end with a smile that says it all.

Never exclude a child from an activity because of his or her disability. Teach up, and he or she will reach up. Create partnerships that are wholesome and self-empowering. Children are great imitators. When you pair your child with an older sibling or family member, the results may exceed your expectations!

Objectives adapted to songs, rhythms, and rhymes are great learning tools. The alphabet song is a great example of teaching a concept through song. I taught the days of the week and the months of the year with a very creative jingle. The students learned the days of the week and the months of the year, in record-breaking time. They eventually recited the same information without music.

The child needs a crutch when the healing is taking place. When the healing is complete, and the crutch is taken away, the child's mind rebounds with an amazing vigor. Songs and informational lyrics act like a crutch until the mind processes and registers the information. Memory triggers are necessary when you're trying to reach a child who's mentally sluggish. If a song triggers the information needed to master an objective, then by all means sing the song and answer the question.

AFTERWARD

Emotional Alienation:
The Child's Social/Emotional Retreat

Slipping into darkness is another way of expressing a child's social/emotional retreat. Some children are reverting backward. Learned behaviors and concepts are fading into the woodwork. Parents swear the child's emotional detachment was not present during the first few years.

What happened to this vibrant child? What caused this sudden detachment to the real world and its surroundings? What caused the learned information to be lost and replaced with confusion, social deprivation, and memory loss? These questions along with many others are being investigated every day.

No one has been able to explain this state of mind. All we know for certain is that this disability exists. More and more of our children are being placed in this category daily. It's still a medical mystery. No one can positively say why this disability is growing at such an alarming rate.

Parents are baffled; they don't know what to do. Books providing information, explanations, educational strategies, and techniques are pretty much nonexistent. Parents are totally caught off guard and are desperately seeking ways to cope with the devastating diagnosis of autism. **I heard your plea.**

Hopefully, my handbook has given you many avenues of coping with the devastating diagnosis of Autism Spectrum. I have outlined valuable methods, strategies, and techniques needed to get maximum productivity. I have supplied you with different methods of sharing and comparing information with your child's pediatrician, teachers, and other support staff. My book has also provided you with instructional advice, learning strategies, and methods of modifying behavior.

Your thirst for knowledge on this subject matter, demonstrates your involvement with your child's education, socialization, revitalization and rehabilitation. Your response reaffirms the purpose of my handbook. **Keep a copy of this handbook with you at all times. It will help you stay one step ahead of the uninformed.**

A special recognition to my assistant, Mrs. Dorothy Mitchell, who serviced my children during my extended illness. I appreciate your loyalty and dedication to our special education students. We couldn't have done it without you!

Thanks again!

Ms. Ethel Williams

APPENDIX I

Remember Your ABCs

A—Assertive Discipline

B—Behavior Modification

C—Commitment

D—Dedication

E—Early Detection

F—Fundamentals of Learning

G—Gather Information

H—High Expectations

I—Intervention (Early)

J—Jump Start (Ignite the learning process)

K—Knowledge (Expand)

L—Language Development

M—Memory Exercises

N—Navigate Your Child's Education

O—Observation

P—Patience, Prayer

Q—Quick response

R—Routine, Repetition, Responsibility

S—Smile Often

T—Teamwork

U—Understanding

V—Victorious

W—Worthy

X—Exercise (large and small muscle groups)

Y—Younger the Better (Identify)

Z—Zealous

Now I know my ABCs, tell me what you think of me!

APPENDIX II

Glossary of Terms

Assertiveness: A method of training individuals to act in a bold self-confident manner (*see reference 1*)

Autism: A severely incapacitating lifelong developmental disability characterized by certain types of behaviors and patterns of interactions and communications. Symptoms include abnormal response to sensation, delayed or absent speech and language, and abnormal ways of relating to people, objects and events. It usually appears during the first three years of life. (*see reference 2*)

Behavior: The manner of conducting oneself (*see reference 1*)

Behavior Modification: Psychotherapy that is concerned with the treatment of observable behaviors rather than underlying psychological processes and that applies principles of learning to substitute desirable responses for undesirable ones, as phobias or obsessions (*see reference 1*)

Discipline: Training that corrects, molds, or perfects the mental faculties or moral character (*see reference 1*)

Fine Motor skills: The precise movement of the small muscles, especially those of the eyes, speech, musculature, hands, fingers, feet, toes. Movement such as blinking, focusing, sucking, grasping, releasing, pinching, and writing are considered to be fine motor activities. Many fine motors skills, including cutting, copying, stringing beads, and tasting require the eyes to direct the hand; these activities are referred to variously as those that require perceptual-motor, visual-motor, and sensory-motor, ocular-motor, or eye-hand coordination. *(see reference 3)*

Gross Motor: Activities that involve the use of the large muscles of the neck, trunk, arms, and legs. Included are basic body movements such as lifting the head, rolling, crawling, creeping, walking, running, leaping, jumping, hopping, galloping, and skipping. Large muscle strength and endurance are also important in climbing, pushing, pulling, hanging, and lifting. (see reference 3)

Manipulatives: Objects (as blocks) that a student is instructed to use in a way that teaches or reinforces a lesson (see reference 1)

Modify: To undergo change; to make basic or fundamental changes. Often to give a new orientation to or to serve a new end *(see reference 1)*

Tactile: Perceptible by touch; relating to, or being the sense of touch (see reference 1)

REFERENCES

1. *Merriam-Webster's Collegiate Dictionary, 11th Edition*, Merriam-Webster, Incorporated, Springfield, Massachusetts, USA

2. Hunt and Marshall (1999), ASD Autism Spectrum Disorder

3. Ruth E. Cook, Diane M. Klein, and Annette Tessier in collaboration with Steven E. Daley, *Children in Adapting Early Childhood Curricula for Inclusive Settings, 6th edition*, Pearson Merrill Prentice Hall, copyright 2004.

4. David R. Goldmann, MD FACP Editor-In Chief-, David A. Horowitz, MD, Associate Editor, *American College Of Physicians Complete Home Medical Guide*, copyrighted 1999 and The American College 2003.